DECISIVE LEADERSHIP: SELF-COACHING TECHNIQUES FOR EFFECTIVE DECISION-MAKING

JEFFREY YEOMANS

Contents

Chapter 1: Understanding Decision-Making

The Importance of Effective Decision-Making for Business Leaders

As a business leader, your ability to make effective decisions is crucial for the success and growth of your organization. Every day, you face numerous decisions that can have a significant impact on the direction and outcome of your business. Therefore, mastering the art of decision-making is essential.

Effective decision-making is not just about making choices; it is about making the right choices. It involves a combination of analytical thinking, intuition, and critical thinking skills. When you make informed and well-thought-out decisions, you minimize risks, optimize resources, and increase the likelihood of achieving your desired results.

One of the key benefits of effective decision-making is improved problem-solving. By using self-coaching techniques, you can develop a structured approach to analyzing problems and generating solutions. This allows you to identify the root causes of issues, evaluate different options, and select the most appropriate course of action. By incorporating self-coaching into your decision-making process, you become more proactive and strategic in addressing challenges, leading to better outcomes for your business.

Another advantage of effective decision-making is the ability to seize opportunities. In today's fast-paced and competitive business environment, opportunities arise and disappear rapidly. As a business leader, you need to be able to evaluate these opportunities quickly and make timely decisions. With the right self-coaching techniques, you can enhance your decision-making speed and accuracy, enabling you to seize opportunities before your competitors do.

Furthermore, effective decision-making instills confidence and trust among your team members and stakeholders. When you consistently make sound decisions, people have faith in your leadership abilities. They trust that you have carefully considered all the factors and made the best choice for the organization. This not only boosts morale but also fosters a culture of trust and collaboration within your team.

Lastly, effective decision-making helps you navigate uncertainty and ambiguity. In today's complex and ever-changing business landscape, leaders often face situations where there is no clear-cut answer or solution. By honing your decision-making skills through self-coaching, you become more comfortable with ambiguity and are better equipped to make informed decisions in uncertain circumstances.

In conclusion, effective decision-making is a critical skill for business leaders. It enables you to solve problems, seize opportunities, build confidence, and navigate uncertainty. By incorporating self-coaching techniques into your decision-making process, you can enhance your analytical thinking, intuition, and problem-solving abilities, leading to better outcomes for your organization. So, invest in developing your decision-making skills and watch your business thrive.

The Challenges of Decision-Making in a Business Context

As business leaders, the ability to make effective decisions is crucial for our success. However, decision-making in a business context can be incredibly challenging. It requires us to consider numerous factors, weigh risks and rewards, and navigate through uncertainty. In this subchapter, we will explore the unique challenges that arise in the realm of decision-making and how self-coaching techniques can help us overcome them.

One of the primary challenges of decision-making in a business context is the abundance of information. As leaders, we are constantly bombarded with data, market trends, and industry insights. This information overload can make it difficult to distill what is truly relevant and make well-informed decisions. Self-coaching techniques can assist us in developing the ability to filter through the noise, identify key information, and make decisions based on accurate and meaningful data.

Another challenge is the pressure to make timely decisions. In the fast-paced business world, time is often of the essence, and delays in decision-making can have significant consequences. This pressure can lead to hasty or impulsive decisions, which may not be well thought out or aligned with long-term goals. Self-coaching techniques can help us develop patience, mindfulness, and the ability to pause and reflect before making important decisions. By cultivating these skills, we can ensure that our decisions are strategic and well-calculated, even within tight timelines.

Furthermore, decision-making in a business context often involves dealing with uncertainty. The future is unpredictable, and we are often faced with ambiguous situations where there is no clear right or wrong answer. This ambiguity can be paralyzing and lead to decision-making paralysis. Self-coaching techniques can help us embrace uncertainty, manage our fears, and develop a mindset that is comfortable with taking calculated risks. By reframing uncertainty as an opportunity for growth and innovation, we can make bold decisions that propel our businesses forward.

Lastly, decision-making in a business context requires considering the perspectives and interests of multiple stakeholders. Balancing the needs of employees, customers, investors, and other stakeholders can be complex and challenging. Self-coaching techniques can help us develop empathy, active listening skills, and effective communication strategies. By understanding and addressing the concerns of various stakeholders, we can make decisions that are inclusive, ethical, and aligned with the overall vision and values of our organization.

In conclusion, decision-making in a business context is fraught with challenges, but by utilizing self-coaching techniques, we can navigate through these challenges more effectively. By developing skills such as information filtering, patience, risk management, and stakeholder consideration, we can enhance our decision-making abilities and drive our businesses towards success. This subchapter will provide practical tools and strategies for business leaders to develop self-coaching skills specifically tailored for decision-making and problem-solving in the fast-paced and ever-evolving business landscape.

The Role of Self-Coaching in Decision-Making

In today's fast-paced and ever-changing business environment, effective decision-making is a crucial skill for business leaders. The ability to make sound decisions can determine the success or failure of an organization. However, with the complexity and uncertainty that often accompanies decision-making, business leaders often find themselves grappling with doubt and indecision. This is where self-coaching techniques come into play, empowering leaders to make confident and effective decisions.

Self-coaching for decision-making and problem-solving is a powerful tool that allows business leaders to navigate through the maze of options and arrive at the best possible outcome. It involves a process of self-reflection, self-awareness, and self-directed learning, enabling leaders to tap into their own knowledge, experiences, and intuition.

One of the key benefits of self-coaching in decision-making is the ability to gain clarity. By asking powerful questions and engaging in reflective practices, leaders can gain a deeper understanding of the situation, their own values, and the potential consequences of their decisions. This clarity helps in eliminating biases and making more objective choices.

Self-coaching also enhances creativity and innovation in decision-making. By exploring different perspectives, challenging assumptions, and thinking creatively, leaders can produce unique solutions to complex problems. It encourages a growth mindset, fostering a culture of continuous improvement and adaptability.

Moreover, self-coaching enables leaders to build resilience in the face of uncertainty. By developing an intense sense of self-confidence and self-trust, leaders can overcome the fear of making wrong decisions. They learn to embrace failure as a learning opportunity and bounce back stronger.

Self-coaching techniques for decision-making are not only applicable to individual leaders but can also be utilized by teams and organizations. It encourages collaboration, communication, and shared learning, leading to more effective and inclusive decision-making processes.

In the book "Decisive Leadership: Self-Coaching Techniques for Effective Decision-Making," business leaders will find an array of practical tools and strategies to enhance their decision-making skills through self-coaching. Each chapter provides step-by-step guidance on various self-coaching techniques, from mindfulness exercises to journaling prompts and scenario analysis.

By incorporating self-coaching into their decision-making processes, business leaders can unlock their full potential, make more informed choices, and drive their organizations towards success in today's dynamic business landscape.

Chapter 2: Self-Awareness and Emotional Intelligence

Understanding Your Decision-Making Style

In the fast-paced and ever-changing world of business, effective decision-making is paramount to success. As a business leader, your decisions can make or break your organization, affecting not just your own future but also the livelihoods of your employees and the overall health of your company. Therefore, it is crucial to understand and cultivate your own decision-making style.

Decisive Leadership: Self-Coaching Techniques for Effective Decision-Making is a comprehensive guide that empowers business leaders like you to develop self-coaching skills for decision-making and problem-solving. This subchapter, "Understanding Your Decision-Making Style," will delve into the importance of recognizing and embracing your unique decision-making style.

Every individual possesses a distinct approach to decision-making, influenced by many factors such as personality traits, past experiences, and cognitive biases. By understanding your decision-making style, you can leverage your strengths, overcome weaknesses, and make more informed and effective decisions.

The first step in understanding your decision-making style is to reflect on your past decisions. Analyze the outcomes, both positive and negative, and identify any patterns or recurring behaviors. This self-reflection will provide valuable insights into your decision-making tendencies and preferences.

Next, it is essential to identify your decision-making biases. Our brains are wired to make shortcuts and rely on cognitive biases when faced with complex decisions. By recognizing these biases, such as confirmation bias or anchoring bias, you can take steps to mitigate their influence and make more objective decisions.

Moreover, understanding your personality traits can shed light on your decision-making style. Are you naturally risk-averse or inclined to take bold risks? Are you more analytical or intuitive in your decision-making process? Recognizing these traits can help you make decisions that align with your strengths and values.

Additionally, considering your emotional intelligence is crucial when understanding your decision-making style. Emotional intelligence allows you to understand and manage your emotions and those of others, enabling you to make decisions with empathy and consideration for all stakeholders.

By understanding your decision-making style, you can leverage it to enhance your leadership skills. Recognizing your strengths and weaknesses will enable you to surround yourself with complementary team members or seek external expertise when necessary. It will also help you adopt a more adaptive approach to decision-making, tailoring your style to various situations.

In summary, understanding your decision-making style is a fundamental aspect of effective leadership. Decisive Leadership: Self-Coaching Techniques for Effective Decision-Making provides you with the tools and insights necessary to identify and cultivate your unique decision-making style. By embracing your style, recognizing biases, and leveraging your strengths, you can become a more confident and decisive business leader, driving your organization towards success.

Assessing Your Emotional Intelligence

In the fast-paced world of business, effective decision-making and critical thinking skills are crucial for success. However, the ability to lead effectively goes beyond just analytical thinking and technical expertise. Emotional intelligence, or EQ, plays a significant role in how business leaders navigate challenges, build relationships, and make decisions that positively impact their organizations.

This subchapter delves into the importance of assessing your emotional intelligence as a business leader and provides self-coaching techniques to enhance this critical skillset. By understanding and developing your EQ, you can elevate your decision-making capabilities and create a more productive and harmonious work environment.

The first step in assessing your emotional intelligence is to recognize the key components that contribute to it. These include self-awareness, self-regulation, motivation, empathy, and social skills. Through a series of self-reflection exercises and assessments, you will gain insights into your strengths and areas for improvement in each of these areas.

Self-awareness is the foundation of emotional intelligence. By understanding your emotions, strengths, and weaknesses, you can make better decisions and manage your reactions more effectively. The subchapter provides practical exercises to enhance self-awareness, such as journaling, mindfulness practices, and seeking feedback from trusted colleagues.

Self-regulation involves controlling your emotions and impulses, especially in high-pressure situations. Techniques like deep breathing exercises, stress management strategies, and reframing negative thoughts can help you develop greater self-control and resilience.

Motivation is essential for driving yourself and others towards success. By aligning your personal and professional goals, setting clear objectives, and fostering a positive work environment, you can cultivate a sense of intrinsic motivation within your team.

Empathy is the ability to understand and relate to the feelings and experiences of others. By actively listening, showing genuine concern, and practicing empathy in your interactions, you can build stronger relationships and create a supportive and inclusive work culture.

Social skills encompass a range of abilities, including effective communication, conflict resolution, and teamwork. Developing these skills can enable you to navigate challenging situations, build strong networks, and collaborate more effectively.

Throughout this subchapter, you will find practical exercises, case studies, and self-assessments to help you evaluate and develop your emotional intelligence. By dedicating time and effort to this process, you can enhance your decision-making abilities, improve your critical thinking skills, and become a more decisive and influential leader.

Remember, emotional intelligence is not a fixed trait and can be developed with practice and self-reflection. By investing in your EQ, you are investing in your own growth as a leader and paving the way for greater success in your career and organization.

Developing Self-Awareness for Better Decision-Making

In today's fast-paced business world, effective decision-making is a critical skill that can make or break a leader's success. To consistently make informed and impactful decisions, business leaders must first develop self-awareness. Self-awareness is the foundation upon which effective decision-making is built, as it allows leaders to understand their strengths, weaknesses, biases, and emotions, enabling them to make more rational and objective choices.

Self-coaching for decision-making and problem-solving is a powerful tool that empowers business leaders to develop self-awareness. By becoming their own coach, leaders can take charge of their decision-making process and enhance their ability to make sound judgments. This subchapter aims to provide business leaders with practical techniques and strategies to develop self-awareness for better decision-making.

The first step towards self-awareness is understanding one's values, beliefs, and goals. By reflecting on these aspects, business leaders can gain clarity on what truly matters to them, enabling them to align their decisions with their core principles. Additionally, identifying personal biases and assumptions is crucial. A leader who is aware of their biases can actively challenge them and consider alternative perspectives, leading to more well-rounded and unbiased decision-making.

Emotional intelligence plays a vital role in self-awareness and decision-making. Recognizing and managing one's emotions enables leaders to remain calm and composed, even in high-pressure situations. By understanding the impact of emotions on decision-making, leaders can effectively separate their feelings from logical reasoning, ensuring more objective decision-making.

Another aspect of self-awareness is understanding one's strengths and weaknesses. By identifying areas of expertise and limitations, leaders can make more informed decisions by leveraging their strengths and seeking assistance in areas where they may lack expertise. Additionally, self-awareness allows leaders to recognize when they need to step back and delegate decisions to others, fostering a collaborative and inclusive decision-making environment.

Self-coaching techniques, such as journaling and self-reflection exercises, can enhance self-awareness for decision-making. Regularly documenting thoughts and experiences can help leaders identify patterns, biases, and areas for improvement. Furthermore, seeking feedback from trusted colleagues or mentors can provide valuable insights into blind spots, enabling leaders to make more informed decisions.

In conclusion, developing self-awareness is essential for business leaders seeking to enhance their decision-making abilities. By understanding their values, biases, emotions, strengths, and weaknesses, leaders can make more rational and objective decisions. Self-coaching techniques, such as reflective exercises and seeking feedback, can enhance self-awareness and lead to better decision-making. With self-awareness as a guiding principle, business leaders can navigate complex challenges with confidence and achieve long-term success.

Chapter 3: Identifying and Defining the Problem

Recognizing the Need for a Decision

In the fast-paced world of business, decision-making is a crucial skill that can make or break a company's success. As a business leader, it is essential to be adept at making effective decisions that can drive growth, solve problems, and navigate through uncertainty. However, recognizing the need for a decision is often the first and most critical step in the decision-making process.

In this subchapter of "Decisive Leadership: Self-Coaching Techniques for Effective Decision-Making," we will explore the importance of recognizing when a decision needs to be made. We will delve into the self-coaching techniques that can help business leaders sharpen their decision-making skills and solve complex problems.

One of the key aspects of recognizing the need for a decision is identifying the existence of a problem or an opportunity. Many business leaders tend to overlook or ignore early warning signs or subtle cues that indicate the need for action. By being proactive and attuned to the environment, you can develop a heightened sense of awareness that allows you to identify potential decision points.

Additionally, self-coaching plays a vital role in recognizing the need for a decision. By cultivating self-awareness and self-reflection, business leaders can better understand their strengths, weaknesses, biases, and blind spots. This introspective process enables leaders to recognize situations where a decision is required and to evaluate their ability to make sound judgments.

Moreover, this subchapter will introduce various self-coaching techniques to enhance decision-making skills. These techniques include mindfulness exercises, journaling, and seeking feedback from trusted advisors or mentors. By incorporating these practices into your daily routine, you can strengthen your decision-making abilities and develop a more agile and analytical mindset.

Furthermore, we will discuss the importance of gathering relevant information and considering multiple perspectives when recognizing the need for a decision. By seeking diverse viewpoints and conducting thorough research, you can ensure that you are making informed choices that align with the needs of your business.

In conclusion, recognizing the need for a decision is a critical skill for business leaders. By being proactive, cultivating self-awareness, and employing self-coaching techniques, you can sharpen your decision-making abilities and become more effective in solving problems and seizing opportunities. This subchapter will provide practical insights and actionable strategies to help you recognize when a decision is needed and equip you with the tools necessary for making well-informed choices.

Analyzing the Problem and its Impact

In the fast-paced world of business, effective decision-making and critical thinking skills are crucial for success. As a business leader, it is imperative to have a clear understanding of the problems you face and their potential impact on your organization. This subchapter aims to guide you through a self-coaching process to analyze problems and evaluate their consequences, empowering you to make informed and decisive choices.

The first step in analyzing a problem is to define it accurately. Take the time to identify the root cause and understand the intricate details. By breaking down the problem into smaller components, you can dissect the issue and gain a comprehensive understanding of its nature. This process enables you to explore different angles and perspectives, ensuring that no crucial aspect is overlooked.

Once the problem is defined, it is essential to assess its impact on your business. Consider the short-term and long-term consequences, both internally and externally. Evaluate how it affects your employees, customers, stakeholders, and the overall performance of your organization. Analyzing the impact allows you to prioritize problems based on their severity and urgency, enabling you to allocate resources effectively.

Furthermore, when assessing the impact, it is vital to consider potential risks and opportunities that may arise from the problem. Sometimes, problems can present unexpected opportunities for growth and innovation. By examining these possibilities, you can turn a challenging situation into a chance to excel.

To analyze the problem and its impact thoroughly, gather relevant data and information. Use both qualitative and quantitative methods to gather insights. This data-driven approach ensures that your analysis is based on facts rather than assumptions. It also helps identify patterns or trends that may have contributed to the problem, enabling you to address underlying issues.

As a business leader, it is crucial to involve your team in the problem analysis process. Encourage open communication and collaboration to gather diverse perspectives. By doing so, you can tap into the collective intelligence of your organization, unlocking innovative solutions and fostering a sense of ownership among your team members.

In conclusion, analyzing the problem and understanding its impact is a vital step in effective decision-making and problem-solving. By defining the problem accurately, assessing its consequences, gathering relevant data, and involving your team, you can make well-informed choices that lead to positive outcomes. This subchapter equips you with self-coaching techniques to navigate the complexities of decision-making, empowering you to become a decisive leader in your industry.

Defining the Problem Clearly and Objectively

In the fast-paced world of business, effective decision-making is crucial for success. Whether you are a seasoned business leader or an aspiring entrepreneur, the ability to make sound decisions is a skill that can be honed through self-coaching techniques. One of the fundamental steps in this process is defining the problem clearly and objectively.

Before embarking on any decision-making journey, it is essential to have a thorough understanding of the problem at hand. This requires a disciplined approach to gather all relevant information, analyze it objectively, and identify the root cause of the problem. By defining the problem clearly and objectively, business leaders can avoid making hasty decisions based on assumptions or incomplete data.

When defining the problem, it is important to ask the right questions. What is the underlying issue? What are the key factors influencing the problem? Are there any patterns or trends that can provide insights? By delving deep into the problem, business leaders can uncover hidden complexities and gain a comprehensive understanding of the situation.

Objectivity is another critical element in problem definition. It is natural for biases and preconceived notions to cloud judgment, but effective decision-makers strive to maintain objectivity. They gather diverse perspectives, seek out contrary evidence, and challenge their own assumptions. By doing so, business leaders can ensure that they are not influenced by personal biases and are open to exploring all workable solutions.

Furthermore, defining the problem objectively allows for a more accurate evaluation of potential solutions. When the problem is clearly defined, it becomes easier to assess the effectiveness of different options. Business leaders can weigh the pros and cons, consider the potential risks and rewards, and make informed decisions based on facts rather than emotions.

Self-coaching for decision-making and problem-solving is a powerful tool for business leaders. By mastering the skill of defining the problem clearly and objectively, they can enhance their decision-making abilities and navigate complex business challenges with confidence. This subchapter of "Decisive Leadership: Self-Coaching Techniques for Effective Decision-Making" provides practical insights and strategies for business leaders to develop this essential skill.

In conclusion, the ability to define the problem clearly and objectively is a critical step in effective decision-making. By asking the right questions, maintaining objectivity, and thoroughly understanding the problem, business leaders can make well-informed decisions that lead to positive outcomes. Through self-coaching techniques, they can refine this skill and become decisive leaders who excel in problem-solving.

Chapter 4: Generating and Evaluating Options

Techniques for Idea Generation

In the fast-paced and ever-evolving world of business, effective decision-making and problem-solving are crucial skills for success. As a business leader, it is essential to constantly generate new and innovative ideas to stay ahead of the competition and drive growth. This subchapter on "Techniques for Idea Generation" aims to provide self-coaching techniques specifically tailored to help business leaders enhance their decision-making abilities and problem-solving strategies.

1. Brainstorming: One of the most well-known techniques for idea generation, brainstorming involves gathering a group of individuals to generate a large number of ideas in a brief period. Encourage an open and non-judgmental environment, allowing participants to freely express their thoughts. This technique promotes creativity and fosters collaboration, leading to fresh perspectives and innovative solutions.

2. Mind Mapping: A visual technique that helps to organize thoughts and ideas. Start with a central

concept or problem and branch out with related ideas, associations, and potential solutions. Mind mapping allows for free-flowing thinking and helps to identify connections between various aspects, leading to new insights and creative solutions.

3. SCAMPER: An acronym for Substitute, Combine, Adapt, Modify, put to another use, Eliminate, and Reverse. SCAMPER is a powerful technique to stimulate idea generation by encouraging the exploration of different possibilities. By manipulating existing ideas through these seven prompts, business leaders can uncover unique perspectives and generate innovative solutions.

4. Role-Playing: This technique involves adopting different perspectives or personas to view a problem from multiple angles. By stepping into the shoes of customers, employees, or competitors, business leaders can gain valuable insights and generate ideas that cater to different stakeholder needs. Role-playing encourages empathy and helps to identify potential roadblocks or opportunities that may not be apparent initially.

5. Random Word Association: This technique involves selecting a random word and brainstorming ideas that relate to it. By forcing connections between unrelated words or concepts, business leaders can break free from conventional thinking

patterns and discover fresh ideas. Random word association encourages thinking freely and facilitates the generation of unique and innovative solutions.

Remember, idea generation is an ongoing process that requires practice and persistence. By incorporating these self-coaching techniques into your decision-making and problem-solving strategies, you will enhance your ability to generate creative ideas, fuel innovation, and make sound business decisions. Embrace the power of these techniques, and watch your business thrive in an increasingly competitive landscape.

Assessing the Feasibility and Risks of Potential Options

In the fast-paced and ever-changing business world, decision-making plays a crucial role in the success of any organization. As business leaders, it is imperative to equip ourselves with effective self-coaching techniques for decision-making and problem-solving. One important aspect of this process is assessing the feasibility and risks of potential options. In this subchapter, we will delve into the importance of this assessment and provide practical strategies to navigate through it.

Feasibility assessment is about determining the practicality and achievability of diverse options under consideration. It involves evaluating the available resources, such as budget, time, and personnel, to determine if they align with the chosen option. By conducting a feasibility assessment, business leaders can identify potential roadblocks and make informed decisions based on realistic expectations.

To assess feasibility, it is crucial to analyze the potential risks associated with each option. Risk assessment enables business leaders to identify potential pitfalls, challenges, and uncertainties that may hinder the successful implementation of a chosen option. By conducting a thorough risk analysis, leaders can develop contingency plans and mitigate potential negative outcomes.

A key strategy for assessing feasibility and risks is conducting a comprehensive SWOT (Strengths, Weaknesses, Opportunities, Threats) analysis. This analysis allows business leaders to identify internal strengths and weaknesses, as well as external opportunities and threats. By understanding these factors, leaders can make more informed decisions and select options that align with their organization's capabilities and goals.

Another valuable technique is scenario planning, which involves creating hypothetical scenarios to explore the potential outcomes of different options. By envisioning various scenarios, business leaders can anticipate potential risks and develop strategies to address them proactively. This approach helps leaders navigate uncertainties and make decisions with a more complete understanding of the potential consequences.

Additionally, seeking input from a diverse group of stakeholders can provide valuable insights and perspectives during the feasibility assessment. By involving individuals from different departments, teams, or even external consultants, business leaders can gain a comprehensive understanding of the potential challenges and risks associated with each option.

In conclusion, assessing the feasibility and risks of potential options is a critical step in effective decision-making. Business leaders must equip themselves with self-coaching techniques to navigate this assessment successfully. By conducting thorough feasibility assessments, analyzing risks, and utilizing strategies such as SWOT analysis and scenario planning, leaders can make informed decisions that align with their organization's capabilities and goals. Furthermore, seeking input from diverse stakeholders ensures a comprehensive evaluation of potential options. With these techniques in hand, business leaders can confidently tackle decision-making challenges and drive their organizations towards success.

Prioritizing and Narrowing Down Options

In the fast-paced and dynamic world of business, decision-making is an essential skill for effective leadership. As a business leader, you are constantly faced with a myriad of options and choices that can significantly impact the success of your organization. However, the ability to prioritize and narrow down these options is crucial to ensure efficient decision-making and problem-solving.

In this subchapter, we will explore the importance of prioritization and provide you with self-coaching techniques to help you effectively narrow down your options when faced with complex decisions.

First, it is vital to recognize that not all options are created equal. To prioritize effectively, you need to identify which options align with your organization's goals and values. Consider the potential outcomes and consequences of each option and evaluate their impact on your business's long-term vision. By focusing on options that are in line with your strategic objectives, you can ensure that your decision-making process remains aligned with your organization's overarching goals.

Once you have identified the most relevant options, it is time to narrow them down further. One effective technique is to conduct a thorough evaluation of the pros and cons of each option. Create a list or a matrix that outlines the advantages and disadvantages of each choice and weigh them against each other. This process will help you gain clarity and make informed decisions based on a comprehensive analysis of the available options.

Another valuable technique for narrowing down options is to seek input from trusted advisors or colleagues. By involving others in the decision-making process, you can gain different perspectives and insights that you may have overlooked. Encourage open and honest discussions and consider the viewpoints of those who have a deep understanding of your industry and market trends. This collaborative approach can help you identify hidden risks and opportunities, leading to more robust and well-rounded decisions.

Furthermore, it is essential to consider the feasibility and resource implications of each option. Assess the financial, human, and time resources required to implement each choice. By considering the practicality of each option, you can eliminate choices that may be unrealistic or financially burdensome for your organization.

Lastly, remember that decision-making is an ongoing process. Keep an open mind and be prepared to adapt and adjust your choices as current information emerges. Stay flexible and agile in your decision-making approach and be willing to revise your priorities if necessary.

In conclusion, prioritizing and narrowing down options is a critical skill for effective decision-making. By aligning options with your organization's goals, evaluating their pros and cons, seeking input from others, considering feasibility, and remaining open to adaptability, you can make well-informed decisions that drive your business towards success.

Chapter 5: Gathering and Analyzing Information

Identifying Relevant Information Sources

As business leaders, the ability to make effective decisions is crucial for our success. To make informed choices, we need to gather relevant and reliable information. However, with the abundance of information available today, it can be challenging to identify the most valuable sources. In this subchapter, we will explore strategies for identifying the right information sources to enhance our self-coaching for decision-making and critical thinking skills.

The first step in identifying relevant information sources is to clearly define the decision or problem at hand. By understanding the specific information, we need, we can narrow down our search and save valuable time. It is essential to establish the key criteria and factors that will influence our decision-making process.

Once we have identified our specific needs, we can turn to a variety of sources to gather information. Traditional sources such as books, industry reports, and academic journals can provide valuable insights and in-depth analysis. These sources often offer a broader perspective and can help us understand the historical context of our decision.

In addition to traditional sources, we must also consider contemporary sources such as online databases, professional networks, and social media platforms. These sources can provide real-time information, industry trends, and expert opinions. However, it is crucial to critically evaluate the credibility and reliability of these sources, as misinformation and biased content can easily spread.

Another valuable source of information is our own network of colleagues, mentors, and industry experts. Engaging in meaningful conversations and seeking advice from those with relevant experience can provide unique insights and alternative perspectives. By leveraging the collective wisdom of others, we can make more well-rounded decisions.

Furthermore, we should not overlook the power of self-reflection and introspection as an information source. Taking the time to reflect on our own experiences, values, and gut instincts can often yield valuable insights. This self-coaching technique allows us to tap into our subconscious knowledge and intuition, which can be invaluable in decision-making.

In conclusion, identifying relevant information sources is a critical skill for business leaders engaged in self-coaching for decision-making and problem-solving. By clearly defining our needs, considering a range of traditional and contemporary sources, leveraging our network, and engaging in self-reflection, we can gather the information necessary to make informed choices. In the ever-evolving business landscape, the ability to identify the right information sources is an essential aspect of decisive leadership.

Collecting and Organizing Information

In the fast-paced and ever-changing world of business, effective decision-making is an essential skill for leaders. The ability to gather and organize information is a crucial step in the decision-making process. In this subchapter, we will explore self-coaching techniques for collecting and organizing information, enabling business leaders to make informed and effective decisions.

Collecting information involves seeking out relevant data and facts. As a business leader, it is essential to identify reliable sources of information, such as industry reports, market research, and expert opinions. Additionally, tapping into the knowledge and expertise of your team members and colleagues can provide valuable insights. By actively engaging in conversations and discussions, you can gather diverse perspectives and challenge your own assumptions.

Once you have collected the necessary information, organizing it in a structured manner is key to effective decision-making. One technique is to create a decision-making framework that outlines the key factors to consider and their relative importance. This framework acts as a guide, ensuring that all relevant aspects are considered. Another approach is to use visual tools, such as mind maps or decision trees, to visually represent the information and its connections. These visual aids can help you identify patterns, relationships, and potential consequences.

In addition to organizing information, it is crucial to evaluate its credibility and reliability. The abundance of information available today makes it necessary to be discerning and critical when assessing its quality. Business leaders should look for evidence-based data, reliable sources, and cross-check information to ensure accuracy and minimize bias. Developing a healthy skepticism and a fact-checking mindset is essential in today's information-rich environment.

Moreover, business leaders should consider the timing of their decision-making process. In some cases, urgent decisions need to be made quickly, while others require a more thorough and deliberate approach. Being able to assess the urgency and importance of a decision will help you prioritize your information collection and organization efforts.

In conclusion, collecting and organizing information is a fundamental aspect of effective decision-making for business leaders. By actively seeking out relevant data and facts, organizing them in a structured manner, and evaluating their credibility, leaders can make informed decisions that have a higher chance of success. Additionally, understanding the timing of decision-making allows leaders to balance the need for speed with the need for thoroughness. By mastering the art of collecting and organizing information, business leaders can enhance their self-coaching for decision-making and problem-solving, leading to better outcomes for their organizations.

Analyzing and Interpreting Data for Informed Decision-Making

In the fast-paced and ever-evolving business world, making informed decisions is crucial for success. As a business leader, you are constantly faced with complex problems and choices that can significantly impact your organization's future. To navigate these challenges effectively, it is essential to rely on data analysis and interpretation to drive your decision-making process.

Analyzing and interpreting data involves collecting, organizing, and evaluating relevant information to gain insights and make informed decisions. It enables you to understand trends, patterns, and correlations that may not be obvious. By harnessing the power of data, you can minimize risks, identify opportunities, and optimize your decision-making process.

One of the key benefits of data analysis is that it allows you to identify and understand the underlying factors influencing a particular issue or problem. By examining various data sources, such as market trends, customer feedback, and financial reports, you can gain a comprehensive view of the situation at hand. This enables you to make decisions based on concrete evidence rather than relying solely on intuition or guesswork.

Interpreting data is equally important, as it involves extracting meaningful insights from the information you have collected. This process requires careful consideration of multiple variables, identifying patterns, and drawing conclusions. Effective interpretation allows you to uncover hidden relationships and trends that can inform your decision-making.

To leverage data analysis and interpretation effectively, business leaders must develop the necessary skills and mindset. This includes being comfortable with quantitative data, understanding statistical methods, and utilizing appropriate tools and technologies. Additionally, it requires fostering a culture of evidence-based decision-making within your organization, where data is valued and utilized throughout all levels.

However, it is important to note that data analysis and interpretation alone are not sufficient for effective decision-making. As a self-coaching technique, it is crucial to combine data-driven insights with your own intuition, experience, and strategic thinking. By integrating these elements, you can make well-rounded decisions that consider both quantitative facts and qualitative considerations.

In conclusion, analyzing and interpreting data is a critical aspect of informed decision-making for business leaders. By embracing data-driven approaches, you can gain valuable insights, mitigate risks, and identify opportunities. However, it is essential to combine data analysis with your own expertise and intuition to make holistic decisions that align with your organization's goals and values.

Chapter 6: Decision-Making Strategies

Rational Decision-Making Model

In today's fast-paced business environment, effective decision-making is crucial for the success of any organization. However, making decisions can often be challenging, especially when faced with complex problems and limited resources. To navigate this terrain successfully, business leaders need a systematic approach that can help them make rational and informed decisions. This subchapter introduces the Rational Decision-Making Model, a proven framework that can enhance your decision-making skills and boost your problem-solving capabilities.

The Rational Decision-Making Model is a step-by-step process that allows business leaders to analyze a situation, generate alternative solutions, evaluate the options, and choose the best course of action. This model is based on the principles of logic, objectivity, and evidence, ensuring that decisions are made based on facts rather than emotions or personal biases.

The first step in the Rational Decision-Making Model is to identify the problem or decision to be made. This involves clearly defining the objective, understanding the context, and gathering all relevant information. By doing so, you can ensure that the decision-making process is focused and aligned with the desired outcome.

Once the problem is identified, the next step is to generate alternative solutions. This requires creativity and brainstorming, as you explore different possibilities and consider multiple perspectives. By encouraging diverse thinking, you can uncover innovative ideas and potential opportunities that might have otherwise been overlooked.

After generating a range of options, it is important to evaluate each alternative objectively. This involves assessing the advantages and disadvantages of each option, considering the potential risks and rewards, and weighing the potential outcomes. By conducting a thorough analysis, you can make a more informed decision and minimize the likelihood of making a poor choice.

The last step in the Rational Decision-Making Model is to select the best alternative and implement it. This involves developing an action plan, assigning responsibilities, and monitoring progress. By following through with the chosen solution, you can ensure that the decision is effectively executed and that the desired results are achieved.

By adopting the Rational Decision-Making Model, business leaders can enhance their decision-making skills and become more effective analytical people. This systematic approach promotes a logical and objective mindset, helping to overcome biases and emotions that can cloud judgment. Moreover, it provides a structured framework that can be applied to various business scenarios, empowering leaders to make sound decisions even in the face of complexity and uncertainty.

In conclusion, the Rational Decision-Making Model is a valuable tool for business leaders seeking to improve their decision-making and problem-solving abilities. By following the steps outlined in this model, leaders can make rational and informed decisions that are based on evidence and logic. This subchapter serves as a guide for self-coaching in decision-making, equipping business leaders with the necessary skills to navigate the challenges of today's business landscape.

Intuitive Decision-Making Model

Subchapter: Intuitive Decision-Making Model

In the fast-paced and ever-changing world of business, effective decision-making is crucial for success. As a business leader, you are constantly faced with making important choices that can impact your organization's bottom line and future trajectory. While there are various decision-making models available, one approach that has gained significant popularity is the Intuitive Decision-Making Model.

Intuition is often described as a gut feeling or an inner voice that guides our choices. Contrary to widespread belief, intuition is not a mystical power but rather a result of our subconscious mind processing vast amounts of information and experiences. By tapping into our intuition, we can leverage this subconscious knowledge to make informed decisions efficiently and effectively.

The Intuitive Decision-Making Model is a self-coaching technique that empowers business leaders to harness their intuition in the decision-making process. This approach recognizes that while logical analysis and data-driven methods certainly have their place, intuition can be an invaluable tool in certain situations. By combining both rational thinking and intuitive insights, leaders can make more well-rounded and informed decisions.

This subchapter will explore the key elements of the Intuitive Decision-Making Model and provide practical strategies for business leaders to incorporate intuition into their decision-making process. It will delve into the following aspects:

1. Understanding the role of intuition: This section will debunk common misconceptions about intuition and explain the science behind its power. It will highlight how intuition can complement logical analysis and provide a competitive advantage in decision-making.

2. Developing intuitive skills: Here, we will discuss techniques and exercises that can help business leaders sharpen their intuitive skills. These can include mindfulness practices, reflection exercises, and learning to trust one's instincts.

3. Balancing intuition and analysis: Effective decision-making requires finding the right balance between intuition and logical analysis. This section will provide practical tips on when to rely on intuition and when to lean on data-driven methods, ensuring a well-informed decision.

4. Overcoming biases and limitations: Intuition is not infallible, and biases can cloud our judgment. This part will explore common biases that can

hinder intuitive decision-making and provide strategies for mitigating them.

By embracing the Intuitive Decision-Making Model, business leaders can enhance their decision-making abilities, solve complex problems more effectively, and gain a competitive edge in today's dynamic business landscape. This subchapter will equip leaders with the necessary tools and techniques to tap into their intuition and make confident decisions that drive their organizations towards success.

Combining Rational and Intuitive Approaches

In the fast-paced world of business leadership, making effective decisions is crucial for success. However, the decision-making process can often be complex and challenging, requiring a combination of rational and intuitive approaches. This subchapter aims to guide business leaders in harnessing the power of both these approaches to enhance their decision-making and critical thinking skills.

Rational decision-making involves a systematic and logical analysis of facts, data, and potential outcomes. It relies on gathering relevant information, weighing the pros and cons, and making an informed choice based on logical reasoning. This approach is essential for making sound decisions in situations that require objective analysis, such as financial planning, resource allocation, or risk assessment.

However, solely relying on rationality can limit a leader's ability to tap into their intuition, which is an invaluable resource for decision-making. Intuition, often described as a "gut feeling" or "sixth sense," is an unconscious process that draws on past experiences, emotions, and patterns to arrive at a decision. It enables leaders to quickly evaluate situations, make snap judgments, and seize opportunities that may not be immediately apparent.

To combine these approaches effectively, business leaders must recognize the strengths and limitations of each. They should start by gathering and analyzing relevant data, utilizing rational decision-making techniques to identify options and assess potential outcomes objectively. This step ensures a solid foundation for decision-making and minimizes biases that can cloud judgment.

However, in complex or ambiguous situations, leaders should also trust their intuition. This requires cultivating self-awareness and learning to listen to their inner voice. By paying attention to subtle cues, gut feelings, and emotional signals, leaders can tap into their intuition to gain valuable insights and consider alternative perspectives that may have been overlooked.

Moreover, fostering an environment that encourages diverse perspectives and open dialogue among team members can enhance decision-making by incorporating multiple viewpoints. By creating a space where rational analysis and intuitive insights are valued equally, leaders can harness the collective intelligence of their team and foster a culture of innovative problem-solving.

In summary, combining rational and intuitive approaches is key to effective decision-making for business leaders. By harnessing the power of both, leaders can make informed choices based on logical analysis while also tapping into their intuition for creative problem-solving. This integration allows leaders to navigate complex and uncertain situations with confidence, ensuring the success and growth of their organizations.

Chapter 7: Making the Decision

Applying Critical Thinking Skills

In the fast-paced and ever-changing business world, effective decision-making is crucial for success. As a business leader, you are constantly faced with complex problems and challenging situations that require your attention. This is where critical thinking skills come into play. Mastering the art of critical thinking can significantly enhance your ability to make informed decisions and solve problems efficiently. In this subchapter, we will explore various techniques and strategies to apply critical thinking skills effectively.

To begin with, critical thinking involves analyzing information objectively and evaluating it from different perspectives. It requires you to question assumptions, examine evidence, and consider alternative solutions. By applying critical thinking skills, you can avoid biases and make decisions based on logical reasoning rather than emotions or preconceived notions.

One key aspect of critical thinking is gathering and analyzing relevant data. As a business leader, you need to ensure that you have access to accurate and reliable information. This may involve conducting research, consulting experts, or utilizing data analytics tools. By thoroughly examining the available data, you can make well-informed decisions that are grounded in facts and evidence.

Another vital component of critical thinking is considering multiple viewpoints. Encouraging diverse perspectives within your team can lead to more comprehensive problem-solving and decision-making processes. By actively seeking input from individuals with diverse backgrounds and expertise, you can uncover blind spots and gain valuable insights. This inclusive approach fosters creativity and innovation while reducing the risk of overlooking crucial details.

Furthermore, critical thinking involves weighing the pros and cons of different options before deciding. This requires a systematic approach to evaluating alternatives, considering potential risks and benefits, and predicting the potential outcomes of each choice. By carefully analyzing the implications of your decisions, you can minimize potential pitfalls and maximize positive outcomes.

Lastly, honing your critical thinking skills requires continuous self-reflection and self-awareness. Recognizing your own biases and limitations is crucial for making objective decisions. Regularly questioning your assumptions, seeking feedback, and challenging your own thinking can help you overcome cognitive biases and broaden your perspectives.

In conclusion, applying critical thinking skills is essential for effective decision-making and problem-solving in the business world. By analyzing information objectively, considering multiple viewpoints, evaluating alternatives, and cultivating self-awareness, you can make well-informed decisions that drive your business forward. Remember, critical thinking is a skill that can be developed and refined over time, and by incorporating it into your self-coaching techniques, you will enhance your leadership abilities and achieve greater success in your decision-making endeavors.

Overcoming Decision-Making Biases and Pitfalls

In the fast-paced world of business, effective decision-making is crucial for success. However, our decisions are often influenced by biases and pitfalls that can hinder our ability to make rational choices. In this subchapter, we will explore some common decision-making biases and pitfalls and provide strategies to overcome them, empowering business leaders to make more informed and effective decisions.

One of the most prevalent biases is confirmation bias, where we seek information that supports our preexisting beliefs and dismiss or ignore evidence to the contrary. To overcome this bias, business leaders must actively seek out diverse viewpoints and perspectives, encouraging a culture of open dialogue and constructive criticism. By considering conflicting information and challenging our assumptions, we can make more well-rounded decisions.

Another common pitfall is the anchoring bias, where we rely too heavily on the initial piece of information received when deciding. To avoid this bias, business leaders should encourage a systematic approach to decision-making, gathering and analyzing all available data before forming a judgment. By considering a broad range of information, we can avoid being overly influenced by a single data point and make more balanced decisions.

The availability bias is also a significant hurdle in decision-making. This bias occurs when we rely on readily available information rather than seeking out more comprehensive and accurate data. To overcome this bias, business leaders should establish a culture of data-driven decision-making, emphasizing the importance of gathering relevant and reliable information to support their choices. By encouraging a thorough examination of all available data, leaders can make more informed decisions that are less influenced by the availability bias.

Furthermore, business leaders must be aware of the sunk cost fallacy, where we continue to invest resources into a failing project or venture based on the amount already invested, rather than its future viability. To overcome this fallacy, leaders should regularly reassess ongoing projects, objectively evaluating their potential for success. By focusing on prospects rather than past investments, leaders can make more rational decisions and allocate resources effectively.

In summary, overcoming decision-making biases and pitfalls is essential for business leaders to make effective choices. By recognizing and addressing biases such as confirmation bias, anchoring bias, availability bias, and the sunk cost fallacy, leaders can navigate through complex decision-making processes with clarity and objectivity. By fostering a culture of open-mindedness, data-driven decision-making, and a focus on prospects, business leaders can enhance their self-coaching for decision-making and problem-solving, leading to improved outcomes and overall success.

Considering Ethical Implications

In the fast-paced and competitive world of business, decision-making is a critical skill that can make or break an organization. Business leaders are constantly faced with complex choices that have far-reaching consequences. However, it is not enough to simply make decisions based on financial feasibility or short-term gains. Ethical implications must also be carefully considered.

Ethics play a vital role in decision-making as they determine what is right or wrong, fair, or unfair. Business leaders have a responsibility to uphold ethical standards and ensure their decisions align with these principles. Failing to do so can lead to damage to the company's reputation, legal issues, and loss of employee trust.

When making decisions, it is important for business leaders to take a step back and evaluate the ethical implications of their choices. This involves considering the potential impact on various stakeholders, including customers, employees, shareholders, and the community at large. It requires a deep understanding of the organization's values and ethical framework.

One ethical consideration that business leaders must address is the potential for conflicts of interest. Leaders should be aware of any personal or commercial interests that may influence their decision-making and take steps to mitigate these conflicts. Transparency and accountability are crucial in maintaining the trust of stakeholders.

Another ethical consideration is the impact on the environment. Sustainable practices and responsible resource management should be integrated into decision-making processes. Business leaders must assess the environmental consequences of their choices and strive to minimize harm.

Additionally, ethical implications extend to the treatment of employees. Leaders must ensure fair and equitable treatment, providing a safe and inclusive work environment. Decision-making should consider the well-being and development of employees, fostering a culture of respect and growth.

Addressing ethical implications requires a strong moral compass and the ability to make difficult choices. It may involve sacrificing short-term gains for long-term sustainability and reputation. Business leaders must lead by example, demonstrating ethical behavior and holding others accountable.

In conclusion, ethical implications are a crucial aspect of decision-making and problem-solving for business leaders. By considering the potential impact on stakeholders, avoiding conflicts of interest, promoting sustainability, and prioritizing employee well-being, leaders can make morally sound choices that benefit both their organizations and society. Ethical decision-making is not only the right thing to do, but it also strengthens the reputation and success of businesses overall.

Chapter 8: Implementing and Communicating Decisions

Developing an Action Plan

In the fast-paced and ever-changing business world, effective decision-making and critical thinking skills are crucial for success. As a business leader, it is imperative to have a well-defined action plan to guide your decision-making process. This subchapter aims to provide you with practical techniques and strategies to develop an action plan that will enhance your self-coaching abilities and enable you to make effective decisions.

To begin with, it is important to understand the key components of an action plan. Firstly, clearly define your objective or the problem you need to solve. This will help you stay focused and ensure that your actions are aligned with your desired outcome. Next, identify the assorted options or solutions available to you. Brainstorming and seeking input from others can be valuable in this stage. Once you have a comprehensive list of options, evaluate each one based on its feasibility, potential risks, and expected outcomes. This evaluation process will enable you to narrow down your choices and select the most suitable option.

When developing your action plan, it is crucial to break down your chosen option into smaller, manageable tasks. This will help you stay organized and ensure that progress is made. Assign specific responsibilities to individuals within your team and set realistic deadlines. By doing so, you can monitor progress and make any necessary adjustments along the way.

Moreover, it is important to consider potential obstacles or challenges that may arise during the implementation of your action plan. Anticipating these obstacles and developing contingency plans will help you navigate through any unexpected hurdles and keep your decision-making process on track.

Another valuable technique for developing an action plan is to prioritize your tasks. Not all tasks are equally important, so it is essential to determine which tasks require immediate attention and which can be addressed later. By prioritizing your tasks, you can ensure that your actions are aligned with your overall objective and make the most efficient use of your time and resources.

In conclusion, developing an action plan is a vital step in effective decision-making and problem-solving for business leaders. By clearly defining your objective, evaluating options, breaking down tasks, anticipating obstacles, and prioritizing your actions, you can enhance your self-coaching abilities and make informed decisions. Remember, a well-developed action plan not only guides your decision-making process but also increases your chances of achieving your desired outcome.

Communicating the Decision Effectively

In the realm of business leadership, effective communication is an indispensable skill that can make or break the success of any decision. Decisions, no matter how well-thought-out or strategically crafted, cannot yield their full potential without proper communication. This subchapter aims to equip business leaders with self-coaching techniques to enhance their decision-making abilities and critical thinking skills through effective communication.

The power of effective communication lies in its ability to inspire, align, and foster understanding among stakeholders. When a decision is made, it is crucial for business leaders to communicate it clearly, concisely, and with conviction. Clarity ensures that everyone understands the rationale behind the decision, while conciseness helps avoid confusion or misinterpretation. Conviction, on the other hand, instills confidence and trust in the decision-maker, fostering a positive environment for implementation.

One self-coaching technique for effective communication is active listening. By genuinely paying attention to others' perspectives, business leaders can gather valuable insights and identify potential concerns or objections. Active listening also demonstrates empathy, which is essential for creating an inclusive and collaborative work environment. Furthermore, it allows leaders to tailor their communication style to cater to the needs and preferences of their audience.

Another technique is adapting the message to different stakeholders. Not all individuals have the same level of knowledge or understanding, so it is important to tailor the message accordingly. By using simple language, relatable examples, and visuals, if necessary, business leaders can ensure that their message is accessible to all. This approach not only increases comprehension but also fosters engagement and promotes a sense of ownership among stakeholders.

Additionally, storytelling can be a powerful tool for effective communication. By sharing relevant anecdotes or case studies, business leaders can create a narrative that resonates with their audience. Stories can captivate attention, evoke emotions, and convey complex ideas in a more digestible manner. This technique not only aids in conveying the decision but also in illustrating its potential impact, making it more relatable and tangible for stakeholders.

Finally, feedback loops are essential for effective communication. Business leaders should create an open and inclusive environment where stakeholders feel comfortable providing feedback and asking questions. This ensures that communication is a two-way street, allowing for clarification, addressing concerns, and adapting the decision if necessary. Regular updates and progress reports also help maintain transparency and accountability throughout the implementation process.

In conclusion, effective communication is a vital component of decision-making and problem-solving for business leaders. By employing self-coaching techniques such as active listening, adapting messages, storytelling, and maintaining feedback loops, leaders can ensure that their decisions are communicated effectively. This not only enhances understanding and alignment but also fosters a positive and collaborative work environment, increasing the chances of successful implementation.

Gaining Buy-In and Support for Decision Implementation

In the fast-paced and competitive landscape of business, making effective decisions is crucial for success. However, the true test of a leader lies not just in making the right decisions but also in gaining buy-in and support for their implementation. Without the support of key stakeholders and team members, even the best decisions can fall flat, leading to a lack of progress and missed opportunities.

This subchapter aims to provide business leaders with valuable insights and self-coaching techniques to navigate the challenges of gaining buy-in and support for decision implementation. By employing these techniques, leaders can increase their chances of successfully executing decisions and ensuring their teams are aligned and committed.

One of the first steps in gaining buy-in is to clearly communicate the decision and its rationale to all stakeholders involved. By articulating the reasoning behind the decision, leaders can help others understand the need for change and how it aligns with the organization's goals. Additionally, leaders must be open to feedback and actively listen to concerns or objections raised by team members. By addressing these concerns and involving others in the decision-making process, leaders can foster a sense of ownership and inclusivity, leading to higher levels of support.

Moreover, leaders must proactively identify potential roadblocks or resistance to change and develop strategies to mitigate them. This subchapter provides self-coaching techniques to help leaders anticipate objections and develop persuasive arguments to counter them. By addressing concerns head-on and highlighting the benefits and opportunities that the decision brings, leaders can win over skeptics and build a coalition of supporters.

Furthermore, understanding the motivations and needs of team members is essential in gaining buy-in. This subchapter explores self-coaching techniques to cultivate empathy and emotional intelligence, enabling leaders to tailor their approach to individuals and address their specific concerns. By demonstrating genuine care and understanding, leaders can build trust and foster a positive environment, making it more likely for team members to support and embrace the decision.

In conclusion, gaining buy-in and support for decision implementation is a critical skill for business leaders. By utilizing the self-coaching techniques presented in this subchapter, leaders can increase their effectiveness in driving change and achieving desired outcomes. By effectively communicating the decision, addressing concerns, and cultivating empathy, leaders can create a sense of shared purpose and commitment, ensuring successful implementation and a united team.

Chapter 9: Reviewing and Learning from Decisions

Evaluating Decision Outcomes and Adjusting Course

In the fast-paced and ever-changing world of business, effective decision-making is crucial for success. As a business leader, you are constantly faced with tough choices that can have significant impacts on your organization. That is where self-coaching for decision-making and problem-solving comes into play, allowing you to navigate through uncertainties and make informed decisions. In this subchapter, we will explore the importance of evaluating decision outcomes and adjusting course, providing you with valuable techniques to enhance your leadership skills.

One of the key aspects of self-coaching is the ability to reflect on your decisions and their outcomes. Instead of dwelling on failures or being overly confident in successes, it is essential to objectively evaluate the results. By analyzing the outcomes, you can identify what worked well and what did not, allowing you to learn from your mistakes and replicate successful strategies in future decision-making processes.

To effectively evaluate decision outcomes, it is crucial to establish clear criteria for success. Define measurable goals and metrics that align with your organization's objectives. By having quantifiable benchmarks, you can assess the impact of your decisions objectively. Additionally, consider involving key stakeholders in the evaluation process to gather diverse perspectives and insights.

Adjusting courses based on evaluation is a critical step towards continual improvement. Sometimes, decisions may not yield the desired outcomes, and it is important to be flexible and adaptive. This subchapter will introduce techniques to help you navigate through such situations. One such technique is the "pivot strategy," which involves analyzing the reasons behind suboptimal outcomes and making necessary adjustments to your decision-making approach. It may involve altering your action plan, reassessing assumptions, or seeking external expertise.

Moreover, this subchapter will emphasize the significance of embracing failure as an opportunity for growth. Failure should not be feared but rather seen as a steppingstone towards success. By adopting a growth mindset, you can learn from your mistakes, adjust your course, and make more effective decisions in the future.

In conclusion, evaluating decision outcomes and adjusting course is a fundamental aspect of self-coaching for decision-making and problem-solving. It enables business leaders to learn from their experiences, make informed decisions, and drive organizational success. By utilizing the techniques and strategies outlined in this subchapter, you can develop a more agile and effective decision-making process, ensuring your organization remains competitive amidst a rapidly evolving business landscape.

Reflecting on Decision-Making Process

In the fast-paced world of business, effective decision-making is crucial for success. Business leaders are constantly faced with important choices that can have far-reaching consequences for their organizations. To make sound decisions, leaders need to develop self-coaching techniques that enhance their decision-making and problem-solving abilities. This subchapter, titled "Reflecting on Decision-Making Process," explores the importance of self-reflection in the decision-making process and provides practical strategies for business leaders to improve their decision-making skills.

Self-coaching for decision-making and problem-solving begins with a deep understanding of one's own decision-making process. By reflecting on past decisions and their outcomes, leaders can identify patterns and biases that may have influenced their choices. This self-awareness is crucial for making more effective decisions in the future. Through self-reflection, leaders can uncover their strengths and weaknesses and learn from their experiences, leading to better decision-making.

One essential strategy for reflecting on the decision-making process is to create a decision journal. This journal serves as a record of decisions, capturing the rationale behind each choice, the alternatives considered, and the outcomes. By reviewing this journal regularly, leaders can identify recurring mistakes or biases and adjust in their decision-making approach. Moreover, it allows leaders to track their growth and progress over time, providing valuable insights into their decision-making skills.

Another useful technique for self-coaching in decision-making is seeking feedback from trusted colleagues or mentors. By soliciting different perspectives, leaders can gain valuable insights and challenge their own biases. Feedback can help identify blind spots, uncover alternative solutions, and broaden the range of possibilities considered during the decision-making process. This process of seeking feedback fosters a culture of continuous learning and improvement.

Furthermore, reflection should not be limited to individual experiences but can extend to analyzing decision-making processes within the organization. By critically examining the decision-making structures and processes in place, leaders can uncover any potential flaws or inefficiencies. This analysis can lead to the implementation of more effective decision-making frameworks that promote collaboration, inclusivity, and creativity.

In conclusion, self-coaching for decision-making and problem-solving is a critical skill for business leaders. By reflecting on their decision-making processes, leaders can uncover biases, learn from past experiences, and continuously improve their decision-making skills. Creating a decision journal, seeking feedback, and analyzing organizational decision-making processes are practical strategies that can enhance the effectiveness of decision-making. Through self-reflection, business leaders can make more informed choices, navigate challenges with confidence, and lead their organizations towards success.

Continuous Improvement for Future Decision-Making

In the fast-paced world of business, effective decision-making is crucial for success. As business leaders, it is essential to constantly strive for improvement in our decision-making abilities. This subchapter explores the concept of continuous improvement and how it can enhance our future decision-making processes.

Continuous improvement is a mindset that encourages us to constantly evaluate and enhance our decision-making skills. It involves a commitment to learning from past experiences, seeking feedback, and adapting our approaches to achieve better outcomes. By adopting a continuous improvement mindset, we can become more effective decision-makers and analytical people.

To begin the journey of continuous improvement, it is important to reflect on our past decision-making processes. This involves analyzing both successful and unsuccessful decisions, identifying the factors that contributed to the outcomes, and understanding the lessons learned. By examining our past decisions, we can gain valuable insights that will inform our future decision-making.

Seeking feedback is another essential aspect of continuous improvement. By actively seeking feedback from colleagues, mentors, and even subordinates, we can gain different perspectives and identify areas for improvement. Constructive criticism can be invaluable in helping us uncover blind spots and address any biases or limitations in our decision-making.

Additionally, continuous improvement requires a commitment to ongoing learning and development. As business leaders, we must stay updated on the latest trends, technologies, and industry best practices. This involves reading relevant books and articles, attending conferences and workshops, and engaging in continuous professional development. By expanding our knowledge and skills, we can make more informed decisions and stay ahead of the competition.

Furthermore, embracing innovation and experimentation is essential for continuous improvement. It is important to challenge conventional wisdom and explore innovative approaches to problem-solving. By taking calculated risks and embracing a growth mindset, we can discover innovative solutions and improve our decision-making abilities.

In conclusion, continuous improvement is a powerful tool for business leaders to enhance their decision-making and critical thinking skills. By reflecting on past decisions, seeking feedback, committing to ongoing learning, and embracing innovation, we can continually improve our ability to make effective decisions. By adopting a mindset of continuous improvement, we can set ourselves apart as decisive leaders in today's competitive business landscape.

Chapter 10: Self-Coaching Techniques for Long-Term Growth

Setting Goals for Developing Decision-Making Skills

In the fast-paced and ever-evolving world of business, the ability to make effective decisions is crucial for success. As a business leader, it is essential to continuously develop and refine your decision-making skills to navigate complex situations and seize opportunities. This subchapter aims to guide you in setting goals that will enhance your decision-making abilities and empower you to become a decisive leader.

Goal 1: Enhance Self-Awareness:
Self-awareness is the foundation of effective decision-making. By understanding your strengths, weaknesses, and biases, you can make more informed choices. Set a goal to regularly assess your decision-making patterns and identify areas for improvement. This could involve seeking feedback from trusted colleagues, reflecting on past decisions, or even engaging in self-coaching

exercises to gain deeper insights into your thought processes.

Goal 2: Expand Knowledge and Expertise
Decision-making is often influenced by the information available. Therefore, it is crucial to continuously expand your knowledge and expertise in your specific industry and relevant fields. Set a goal to dedicate time each week to stay updated on industry trends, attend conferences or workshops, and engage in professional development activities. By broadening your knowledge base, you will be better equipped to make well-informed decisions.

Goal 3: Develop Critical Thinking Skills
Critical thinking is an essential component of effective decision-making. Set a goal to enhance your critical thinking skills by regularly engaging in exercises that challenge your assumptions and encourage you to consider alternative perspectives. This could involve solving complex problems, participating in brainstorming sessions, or even seeking out diverse opinions within your team or network.

Goal 4: Foster a Decision-Making Culture
As a business leader, it is not only your individual decision-making skills that matter but also the decision-making culture within your organization. Set a goal to foster an environment that encourages

open dialogue, collaboration, and shared decision-making. This could involve implementing practices such as regular team meetings, structured decision-making processes, and creating opportunities for employees to contribute their ideas and insights.

Goal 5: Embrace Risk and Learn from Failure
Making bold decisions often involves taking risks. Set a goal to embrace calculated risks and learn from both successes and failures. Encourage a growth mindset within yourself and your team, where failures are seen as opportunities for learning and improvement. By embracing risk and learning from failures, you will become more comfortable with making tough decisions and develop resilience in the face of challenges.

By setting these goals and actively working towards them, you will develop the necessary skills and mindset to become a decisive leader. Remember, effective decision-making is a continuous journey, and by investing in your self-coaching for decision-making and problem-solving, you will not only enhance your own performance but also create a positive impact on your team and organization.

Self-Reflection and Journaling

In the fast-paced world of business, decision-making is a crucial skill that can make or break a company's success. As a business leader, it is imperative to develop effective strategies for decision-making and problem-solving. One highly effective technique that can assist in this process is self-reflection and journaling.

Self-reflection is the process of introspection, examining one's thoughts, emotions, and actions to gain a deeper understanding of oneself and the decisions made. It allows business leaders to evaluate their strengths, weaknesses, and biases, providing valuable insights that can enhance decision-making capabilities.

Journaling, on the other hand, is a practical tool that complements self-reflection. It involves the act of writing down thoughts, ideas, and experiences in a structured manner. By keeping a journal, business leaders can document their decision-making processes, record the outcomes, and reflect on the lessons learned along the way.

Self-reflection and journaling work hand in hand to create a powerful self-coaching technique for decision-making and problem-solving. When used consistently, they can offer a number of benefits to business leaders:

1. Enhanced Self-Awareness: Self-reflection and journaling allow business leaders to gain a deeper

understanding of their own values, beliefs, and biases. This heightened self-awareness enables them to make more conscious and informed decisions, ensuring alignment with their personal and organizational goals.

2. Improved Clarity: By regularly documenting thoughts and ideas in a journal, business leaders can clarify their thinking processes. This clarity helps them identify patterns, make connections, and derive insights that may have otherwise gone unnoticed. It leads to more effective problem-solving and decision-making.

3. Emotional Intelligence Development: Self-reflection and journaling provide an opportunity for business leaders to explore and manage their emotions. By examining the emotional aspects of decision-making, they can develop emotional intelligence, enabling them to make more empathetic and balanced choices.

4. Continuous Learning: Through self-reflection and journaling, business leaders can create a repository of valuable insights and experiences. This knowledge base serves as a resource for continuous learning, allowing them to build upon past successes and failures and make better-informed decisions in the future.

In conclusion, self-reflection and journaling are powerful self-coaching techniques that can significantly enhance decision-making and critical thinking skills for business leaders. By incorporating these practices into their daily routine, leaders can cultivate self-awareness, gain clarity, develop emotional intelligence, and engage in continuous learning. These techniques empower business leaders to make decisive and effective choices, driving their organizations towards success in a rapidly changing business landscape.

Seeking Feedback and Mentorship

In the fast-paced and ever-evolving world of business, effective decision-making and critical thinking skills are paramount for success. As a business leader, it is crucial to continuously develop and refine these skills to stay ahead of the competition. One powerful technique that can enhance your decision-making abilities is seeking feedback and mentorship.

Feedback is a valuable tool that provides insight into your blind spots and areas for improvement. By actively seeking feedback from your team, colleagues, and even clients, you can gain a fresh perspective on your decision-making process. This feedback not only helps you identify any biases or pitfalls that you may have overlooked but also helps you learn from your mistakes and make better decisions in the future.

One effective way to seek feedback is through regular performance evaluations or 360-degree assessments. These assessments involve gathering feedback from multiple sources, including superiors, subordinates, and peers. By involving a diverse range of perspectives, you can gain a comprehensive understanding of your strengths and weaknesses, enabling you to make more informed decisions.

Additionally, seeking mentorship from experienced professionals can provide invaluable guidance and support in your decision-making journey. Mentors can offer valuable insights based on their own experiences, helping you navigate complex business challenges with confidence. A mentor can also serve as a sounding board for your ideas and provide constructive feedback, allowing you to refine your decision-making skills further.

When seeking a mentor, it is important to choose someone who aligns with your values, possesses the expertise you seek, and is willing to invest time and energy in your development. Finding a mentor within your industry or professional network can provide you with specific insights and knowledge that are directly applicable to your decision-making processes.

However, do not limit yourself to seeking feedback and mentorship only within your immediate circle. Consider joining professional organizations, attending industry conferences, or even seeking virtual mentorship through online platforms. These opportunities can expose you to a wealth of knowledge and diverse perspectives that can positively impact your decision-making abilities.

In conclusion, seeking feedback and mentorship is a crucial aspect of self-coaching for decision-making and problem-solving. By actively seeking feedback from various sources and finding a mentor who can guide you, you can enhance your decision-making skills and stay ahead in the competitive business world. Embrace the power of feedback and mentorship, and watch your decision-making abilities soar to new heights.

Conclusion: Empowering Business Leaders through Self-Coaching for Effective Decision-Making.

Conclusion: Empowering Business Leaders through Self-Coaching for Effective Decision-Making

In today's fast-paced, ever-changing business landscape, effective decision-making is crucial for success. As business leaders, you are constantly faced with complex challenges and critical choices that can determine the future of your organization. To navigate this complex terrain, self-coaching techniques for decision-making and problem-solving become invaluable tools in your arsenal.

Throughout this book, "Decisive Leadership: Self-Coaching Techniques for Effective Decision-Making," we have explored the power of self-coaching and its impact on business leaders. We have delved into various self-coaching methodologies, strategies, and exercises that can enhance your decision-making abilities, allowing you to make informed choices and overcome obstacles with confidence.

One of the key takeaways from this book is the importance of self-awareness in decision-making. By developing a deep understanding of your strengths, weaknesses, values, and biases, you can gain clarity and objectivity in your decision-making process. Through self-reflection exercises and techniques, you can uncover hidden biases, challenge assumptions, and expand your perspectives. This heightened self-awareness will enable you to make more effective decisions, free from personal biases and limiting beliefs.

In addition to self-awareness, this book has emphasized the significance of critical thinking and critical thinking skills. As a business leader, you must be able to analyze complex situations, evaluate potential solutions, and choose the most appropriate course of action. Through self-coaching techniques such as SWOT analysis, decision trees, and scenario planning, you can enhance your analytical thinking and problem-solving abilities, enabling you to make more robust and well-informed decisions.

Furthermore, this book has highlighted the importance of emotional intelligence in decision-making. As a business leader, your decisions can have a profound impact on your team and stakeholders. By cultivating emotional intelligence through self-coaching exercises, such as self-regulation, empathy building, and active listening, you can navigate interpersonal dynamics and make decisions that resonate with your team, fostering a culture of trust, collaboration, and engagement.

In conclusion, the power of self-coaching for effective decision-making cannot be overstated. By developing self-awareness, honing critical thinking and critical thinking skills, and nurturing emotional intelligence, you can empower yourself as a business leader to make confident, well-informed decisions that drive success and growth. The techniques and strategies explored in this book are practical, actionable, and tailored to the unique challenges faced by business leaders like you. Embrace self-coaching as a lifelong learning journey and watch as your decision-making abilities soar to new heights, propelling your organization towards a prosperous future.

The Author

Jeffrey Yeomans is an accountability and Leadership Life Coach specializing in leading people. He has been supporting leadership development and daily productivity for over 24 years.

Over the last 15 years I have completed extensive research around business coaching and life coaching for workers. Since I started in leadership, I have noticed a definite change in leadership styles and the development of coaching and training modeled around employees.

I have worked in various industrial plants for the last 35 years. Like many people in a technical environment, I advanced up the ladder mainly because of my technical skills and my willingness to take on more responsibility. It was only after I became a supervisor that I realized I needed to improve my leadership skills.

As I searched for training material related to coaching and leadership, I have combined all this learning and my experimentation with clients to form this self-coaching system. I designed it for people who cannot afford a professional coach.

Jeffreyyeomans.com

The Self Coaching Exercises

This is the section of the book where you should print out the questions so that you can record your answers.

The simple questions used in this personal self-growth coaching program require that you answer them truthfully and completely to provide the results you are looking for. From experience the self-administered model is effective in helping you obtain small to medium goals.

If you require additional assistance for larger and complex goals, then we suggest you engage a life or business coach to assist you in the full process.

Step 1:

Important goals that I want to achieve:

1._____

2._____

3._____

4._____

5._____

6._____

Goal questions (ask Yourself for each goal above)

What are the goals I want to achieve?
_____

Why am I hoping to achieve this goal?
_____

Who else needs to know about the plan?
_____

How will I inform them? _____

What do I want more of in my life? _____

What would I try now if I knew I could not fail?
_____

What am I aiming for in the long/medium/short term?

When would I like to have reached this goal? _____

How will I know when I have achieved this goal?
_____

What will it look/feel/sound like?

_____

What could I do today that would make the biggest difference to my life? _____

Step 2:

Out of all goals, this one is the most important to me (complete rest of exercise with this primary goal): _____

Step 3:

Break down your goal into small actions, steps, and groups of tasks.

Step 4:

Based upon these smaller tasks, how long will it take me to achieve this goal: _____

Do I commit 100% to achieve this goal: ☐YES ☐NO

Reward I will give to myself once I achieve this goal: _____

Reality questions (ask Yourself)

What do I see is happening now around me (this issue)?

What have I done so far towards this (goal)?
_____

What is my main concern around this goal/issue?

What resources do I have to help me with this?
_____

What might be holding me back? _____

Why haven't I reached that goal already? _____

What do I think is stopping me? _____

What do I think other people's perception of the situation is?

Do I know other people who have achieved that goal?

What have I already tried?
_____

How could I turn this around this time? _____

What could I do better this time? _____

On a scale of 1-10 how severe/serious/urgent is the situation?

How is the current situation affecting me, others, my overall life?

What are the factors I need to consider?

_____

Do I need anyone else to participate in this conversation?

How urgent is this situation to me? _____

How will my success/failure at addressing this affect the rest of my life or business? _____

Who else do I believe shares my concerns and needs to find a solution? _____

How will I know I have this managed?

_____

Step 5:

Strengths I have that can help me to achieve this goal:

1._____

2._____

3._____

"Options" questions

What could I do to move myself one step closer to achieving my goal? _____

What are all the unusual ways I could approach this? _____

What else could I do? _____

What if I knew that I could not fail? _____

If I could think of three more things, what would they be?

What else could I do? What else? Anything else? What next?

What could be my first step? _____

Who else might be able to help? _____

What would happen if I did nothing? _____

What has worked for me already? _____

How could I do more of that? _____

What would I suggest to a friend in a comparable situation? _____

What would happen if I did that? _____

What is the hardest/most challenging part of that for me? _____

What advice would I give to a friend about that challenge? _____

What would I gain by doing/saying that? _____

What would I lose by doing/saying that? _____

If someone did/said that to me, what do I think would happen? _____

What is the best/worst thing about that option? _____

Which option do I feel ready to act on? Scale 1-10 what is this option? _____

"Will" questions

Which of my options feels, seems, looks, and sounds the best?

Which would take me closer to my long-term goal?

Which would give me the most satisfaction?
_____

On a scale of 1-10, how committed am I to this goal?

What would need to happen to prove I have achieved this goal?

Who do I need to talk to first? Who needs to know?

What would increase my success rate? (e.g., manage fear, clearer steps, more support, etc.)
_____

What will happen (what is the cost) of NOT doing this?

How will I know if this is completed satisfactory?

How am I going to do this? _____

What is the first step?

When will I take the first step? _____

Could anything stop me?

What are the risks? _____

Step 6:

Which actions do I need to take to achieve this
goal? Analyze this goal and break it down into
smaller actionable tasks. If a goal cannot be broken
down into tasks, it is too general:

Action 1: _____

Action 2: _____

Action 3: _____

Action 4: _____

Tactic questions

How and when will I do this? _____

What is my plan to do this? _____

What support do I need to get this done? _____

What are 3 actions I can take that would make sense to do today?

What are 3 actions that I can take this week?

On a scale of 1-10, how excited do I feel about taking these actions?

What do I need from myself or others to help me achieve this?

How will I know when I have done it? _____

Who will I involve in this? _____

When will I do this? _____

Specifically what actions will I take and when will I carry them out?

What specific step will I take next?

How will that help me reach my goal?

Here are some additional tips for tactical development. You can use these tips to help give you more ideas.

Identify your Needs - Identify your needs in ways that you will understand. Create actions that will help you reach your goal.

Establish Your Success Metrics - based on growth evaluation, having a measurement for your success allows you to measure the effectiveness of your actions and plans.

Understand the Investments -

PERSONAL COSTS - What will be the personal costs to these actions and changes in my life? How will I deal with both positive and negative costs that result from my actions? _____

PROCESS COSTS - What is the total cost of this process? Are the benefits I will obtain from reaching my goals and the changes made in my life worth the cost of engaging in the process? _____

HIDDEN COSTS - Have I missed any hidden costs that I should be considering? What would I do if a cost that I was not aware of shows itself? _____

Step 7:

Habits - Things I choose to start doing and stop doing which will help me achieve my goal:

START DOING

1. _____

2. _____

3. _____

4. _____

5. _____

STOP DOING

1. _____

2. _____

3. _____

4. _____

5. _____

Habit Questions

What are some good habits that I already have that can help you reach your goal? _____

What habits do you need to change to obtain your goal?

What is your plan to sustain your success? _____

Can you break this plan down into manageable steps?

Can you sustain each of these steps until they become an involuntary activity (30 days)? _____

What activities are you going to have to give up allowing for the new habit to be developed?
_____

Are you committed to changing the habit?

Will you tell others about the new habit you are trying to form and why you are doing it? _____

Can you develop an affirmation around this habit to remind yourself of its importance to your success?
_____

Step 8:

Which new skills/knowledge will help me achieve my goal?

1._____

2._____

3._____

4._____

5._____

When you are looking at a new habit or action, do not be afraid of taking that first step. Ask yourself; "what is the worst thing that could happen" for every action that you are nervous about or reluctant to take. Then proceed to answer that question for each action.

After you have thought about the worst thing that could happen, flip that question on its lid and ask yourself "what is the best thing that could happen" if I take this action.

Get into a habit of flipping any negative thinking into positive thinking when looking at your actions. There is always good and bad in everything we do, so if you focus on the positive outcome of the action, you are more likely to take that step towards your goal.

The actual worst thing that can happen is never as bad as you think when you really analyze it. There are very few actions for improving your life that will cause you serious physical or mental harm.

We may think an action is risky but when we really look at it objectively, much of the reluctance is just in our mind. Change is never easy, but if you can work through those negative thoughts, you are well on your way towards your goal.

Step 9: My progress:

What is working well (accomplishments)

- _____

- _____

- _____

- _____

- _____

What do I need to change (improve)

- _____

- •_____
- •_____
- •_____
- •_____

Step 10:

Who can help me achieve this goal faster?

When you have finished this complete self-coaching exercise, you will have determined your primary goal and a process to bring it to completion. The results you can get from following this self-directed coaching model will be equal to the effort you put into following the process.

Many people have used this same process to bring about life-changing growth in their life. Whether your personal life goal is losing weight or finding a new career, the process will be the same. This is also true for business related goals.

As stated above this Personal Self Growth Results Coaching exercise is suitable for small to medium sized goals.

When you are self-coaching, it is best to focus on one goal or result at a time.

If you have a more complex goal that requires completing multiple steps you may want to consider using a personal life coach. A life coach is trained in helping people get the best results for larger projects.